Penguin Books/The Battle of Bogside

Clive Limpkin was born in 1937 and educated in Beckenham. He left school to train in forestry for three years, interrupted by National Service in the RAF in Germany. He started working as a writer and photographer with a literary agency for sportsmen in Fleet Street and in 1967 joined the *Daily Express* as a photographer. It was in 1969 when he moved to the *Daily Sketch* that he was first sent to Ulster, and has been covering the troubles ever since. For the past two years he has been a staff photographer with the *Sun*. Clive Limpkin is married to a hotelier in Surrey.

Clive Limpkin

The Battle of Bogside

PENGUIN BOOKS

To Alex, for her love and encouragement

Penguin Books Ltd, Harmondsworth,
Middlesex, England
Penguin Books Inc., 7110 Ambassador Road,
Baltimore, Maryland 21207, U.S.A.
Penguin Books Australia Ltd, Ringwood,
Victoria, Australia

Published in Penguin Books 1972

Made and printed in Great Britain by
Hazell Watson & Viney Ltd,
Aylesbury, Bucks
Set in Monophoto Plantin

Acknowledgements

For the use of the photographs, taken by the author, on pages 10–11, 12, 13, 14, 15, 16–17, 18–19, 20–21, 22, 23, 24, 25 26–7, 27, 28–9, 29, 30–31, 31, 32–3, 34–5, 36–7, 37, 38, 39, 40, 40–41, 42–3, 44–5, 46–7, 48–9, 49, 50–51, 52, 53, 54, 54–5, 55, 56, 57, 58, 59, 60, 60–61, 61, 62–3, 64, 65, 66–7, 68, 69, 94, 128, 129, 132, 166, we wish to thank the Associated Newspaper Group Limited. The copyright is the property of the Associated Newspaper Group Limited.

We also wish to thank the *Sun* newspaper for the use of photographs, taken by the author, on pages 72–3, 78–9, 84, 85, 90, 91, 95, 96, 96–7, 101, 108, 109, 115, 122–3, 135, 138, 139, 140–41, 142–3, 148–9, 151, 154–5, 158–9, 160–61, 162–3, 163, 168. The copyright is the property of the *Sun*.

All other photographs in this book are the copyright of Clive Limpkin.

We should like to thank the darkroom staff of Associated Newspapers and the *Sun* for their co-operation in the production of this book.

All photographs were taken with Nikon F cameras with lenses ranging from 24 mm. to 300 mm., using Ilford HP4 film and printed on Ilfobrom paper.

Introduction

These photographs of the fighting in Derry were all taken while covering the troubles in Northern Ireland as a staff photographer for the *Daily Sketch* in 1969, and subsequently for the *Sun*. I don't pretend they are a comprehensive record of the period; in exposure time they represent only three seconds in the three years they cover. At best, they can only be an impression of the impasse reached.

If a bias is read into the pictures or words, then I hope it is for the moderate majority of Northern Ireland, both Catholic and Protestant, who have inherited this awful problem and live in hope of solving it peacefully.

Compared with Vietnam or Pakistan, Ulster is no more than a scratch, a local irritation. But it doesn't lessen the madness. It is still a war.

London
August 1972

The Problem

It is too easy to say that the Ulster problem is a religious war between Catholics and Protestants; a war of Christians fighting Christians in the name of Christ. It is also a colonial war, fought between the Protestant settlers, planted by the English conquerors centuries ago, and the native Catholics.

The Catholics, it is said, are blacks who happen to have white faces. And, like the poor whites of America who persecute the blacks, it is the poor Catholic who suffers at the hands of his Protestant counterpart.

Though the problem began centuries ago, it survives today because bigotry, persecution and mistrust have been handed down to each successive generation with a fervour that only religion can create. The children learn to hate before they've learnt to read.

But to follow the tortuous history that has led the Irish to the present situation is, as Lloyd George said, like trying to pick up mercury with a fork. Basically, after 400 years of sporadic and unsuccessful attempts to conquer Ireland, an English Army, in 1601, defeated the last of the great Irish Catholic earls. Their lands were turned over to the English, who brought in Scottish Protestant settlers to colonize the land and control the native Catholics. Bloodshed has continued ever since in the native's struggle to rid his country of these colonists.

In 1690 England's King James II (a Catholic convert) was defeated by the Calvinist William of Orange, his successor. There followed in Ireland penal laws which increasingly oppressed and persecuted the natives. Catholic rights to land ownership, education and positions of administration were progressively curtailed. It was the persecution of a majority which has continued ever since.

In 1800 William Pitt, the British Prime Minister, successfully abolished the Irish Parliament and, to the horror of the Catholics, replaced it with direct rule from Westminster.

In 1858 a group of Irish nationalists formed the Irish Republican Brotherhood. It was a weak, romantic movement, but it gave birth to the militant Irish Republican Army, the IRA, which on Easter Monday, 1916, declared Ireland a republic. The movement was crushed by the British Army, but it was followed by years of guerilla war between the Irish and British, resulting in 1921 with the fateful partition of Ireland in which the 26 southern counties, mainly Catholic, became the Irish Free State and the 6 northern counties, dominated by Protest-

ants, became the British province of Northern Ireland, to be known as Ulster.

From the start it was an anomaly, an experiment that could never succeed. Ulster was to be part of the United Kingdom, and yet self-governed (by a Northern Ireland Parliament at Stormont).

It was born with the burden of an economic slump from which it has never recovered. The industrial pattern that existed was archaic, largely controlled by great industrial families fiercely tied to the Tory establishment. It was they who instigated the discrimination, particularly in manpower, which survives today along with a vast unemployment problem and acute poverty for both Catholic and Protestant working class alike.

Worse still, one third of the new Ulster province was Catholic and violently opposed to becoming part of the United Kingdom, and therefore British; they wanted to be Irishmen and part of a self-governing United Ireland. It meant that the ruling Protestants looked upon one citizen in three as unacceptable politically and therefore not entitled to the full citizen's rights and privileges of the remaining two-thirds 'loyalist' population. So the deprivations continued.

Yet the feelings of these Protestants is understandable. They had no wish to be ruled by Catholics from Dublin, nor lose their British status. Whatever persecution had been committed by their forebears, should they pay for it now as a generation by being governed by a foreign parliament? And with the high Catholic birthrate, the fear of being outbred has always been at the back of the Protestant's mind.

In this unworkable situation the frustration and violence of both sides has never been far below the surface. It needed one spark to start the violence. And that spark was to come on 12 August 1969, in Derry, a divided city in a divided Ulster in a divided Ireland.

It was in 1689 that the City of Derry held out against a 15-week siege by 20,000 French and Irish troops under the Catholic James II before successful relief. But it was an incident prior to the siege, in which 13 apprentice boys held the Ferryquay Gate on the City's walls against the troops, that is so venomously remembered by the Protestants on 12 August each year.

And it was beneath these city walls that Catholics had settled on bog land; an area which came to be known as Bogside.

It is hard for the outsider to imagine the fervour that this Protestant victory, 280 years old, can create; but what is history to the world is fuel to the Irish.

Nowhere in Northern Ireland is the Protestant

domination more brazenly demonstrated than in Derry on 12 August, when thousands of Protestants marched to pipe, drum and flute bands to celebrate. They sang songs of victory, firing cannon from the city walls over the Bogside ghetto beneath, where nearly 20,000 Catholics lived in squalid housing, with an unemployment figure of 1 in 4, a majority of 2 to 1 – and little else.

It is not hard to imagine the effect it had on the Catholics. They lived under a system of local government in which, as late as 1966, gerrymandering of ward boundaries could produce a city council of 12 Protestants and 8 Catholics in a city which had a population of 14,000 Catholic and 9,000 Protestant voters.

Worse still, the housing system allowed local councils legally to refuse Catholics houses outside Catholic wards. (In fact, to ensure this, Derry's housing programme up to 1969 was actually reduced.)

Bogside itself was policed, like the rest of Northern Ireland, by the Royal Ulster Constabulary, the RUC, a totally Protestant force in a totally Catholic area in a religiously divided country. Derry, in fact, was under a feudal system which it was difficult to believe had survived the nineteenth century, let alone reached 1969.

Yet the 1969 troubles might be traced to 5 October 1968, when the comparatively small Northern Ireland Civil Rights Association (NICRA) planned a march into the Protestant city centre. The march was banned by Stormont, the ban was defied, and the marchers reached the centre before an RUC baton charge broke them up.

For the first time the Protestant city had been breached, the TV cameras were there to witness the ugly baton charge, with blows aimed at heads and genitals. It was a day which spotlighted NICRA and their grievances, and had shown to senior RUC officers that in the increasingly likely event of a larger march, they would be outnumbered.

As a result of the march, Stormont passed a reform programme in an attempt to appease NICRA, now growing into a mass movement. To the Catholics, these reforms were too weak, to the Protestants they were too strong, proof to them of their government's submission to these agitators.

Then, in January 1969, the newly formed People's Democracy movement held a civil rights march from Belfast to Derry. At Burntollet Bridge, a few miles from Derry, the marchers were ambushed by Protestant extremists (including, it was later discovered, members of the RUC's reserve force, the B Specials). They used cudgels, bottles and stones; even girl marchers were thrown into a near-by river and beaten. Again TV cameras were there,

recording it all. The world was seeing, possibly for the first time, that such violence could be created by politics and religion within the United Kingdom. On 4 January, when the march finally reached Derry, there were claims of RUC brutality against the Catholics. It brought the decision that with feelings so high, the RUC would stop patrolling the Bogside.

That decision, a genuine bid for temporary peace, was to have far-reaching repercussions, for it was the virtual birth of Free Derry, a no-go area combining the Bogside and Creggan districts of Derry, where police (and later British troops) declined to patrol; a lawless area of the United Kingdom, where peace was in the hands of the inhabitants and which was to become a painful embarrassment to Westminster, and a massive lever to the Catholic and IRA who later came to rule it.

There followed a summer of brittle peace, so easily punctured by violence that the impending 12 August march was becoming more and more significant to both Protestant and Catholic.

To the Protestants, suffering from world condemnation of the Burntollet Bridge ambush and the subsequent RUC violence, the Apprentice Boys' march would be a vital fillip to their morale. But to the Catholics, now convinced of the RUC's total partiality towards the Protestants, the march threatened a Protestant – even police – invasion of the Bogside. Worse still, it might lead to the Protestant pogrom that generations of them had feared.

To meet these fears, the Catholic's middle-of-the-road Derry Citizen's Action Committee led by local MP, John Hume, was replaced by the more militant Derry Citizen's Defence Association, (DCDA) with IRA membership. Its first aim was to organize the defence of Bogside; it immediately showed itself capable of the task, arranging first-aid stations, its own ambulance and fire service, and the erection of barricades across key roads leading into the Bogside.

Robert Porter, Northern Ireland's Minister of Home Affairs, had to make the fateful decision whether to allow the march to continue or not. To control the march, he had at his disposal the RUC (with an overall strength of 3,200), which normally was supported by the Ulster Special Constabulary, the B Specials, a reserve force of 8,500. But this Protestant part-time force was hated by the Catholics for their alleged brutality and aggression; to involve the B Specials in possible sectarian fighting was out of the question.

As a last resort, Porter had the power to call in the Army, but their arrival would raise great problems, they would probably create more trouble than they could resolve, and they would remain under the control of Westminster, surely only one step away from Direct Rule.

Trouble seemed inevitable with the march's route to the edge of the Bogside, but to cancel it, he was warned by Protestants, could itself lead to Protestant riots.

To Porter, the stewarding by the Protestants and Catholics on the day was vital. The Protestants promised him sufficient stewarding to maintain control of their marchers. From the Catholic DCDA he received the assurance that their stewarding was efficient and well planned. It was this assurance that proved crucial. For Porter believed the DCDA to be saying that their stewarding was sufficient for the prevention of trouble. It wasn't: it was only sufficient for the defence of the Bogside.

On the strength of these assurances Porter decided to allow the march to take place. It was a decision that was to spark off the riots that have continued ever since. Blessed with the gift of hindsight, so many critics have condemned it as the wrong decision. It was, but only because there wasn't a right one for Porter to make – a situation which has faced politicians involved in the Irish situation for centuries.

And when the day came, as the 15,000 marched through the city, some Protestants threw pennies over the City wall into the Bogside below.

For the Bogsiders, persecuted and deprived for 300 years, breaking point had been reached. When the trouble came, it was, predictably, as the march reached the edge of the Bogside. First a few nails were thrown at the Protestants, then one man fired a marble from a catapult. Within minutes Waterloo Place was a battleground, with the Bogsiders stoning and petrol-bombing the RUC, fighting back down William Street, towards the barricades. On the roof of Rossville flats, crate upon crate of petrol bombs was lined up, awaiting the first attack.

It was the start of five days of almost continuous bloody rioting that in the eyes of the Protestants was proof that the IRA was behind the Civil Rights movement, but to the Catholics confirmed that the RUC were party to the Protestant pogrom they had dreaded.

Both convictions were false, but in that terrible atmosphere of mistrust both were plausible and understandable. It was five days, in fact, that put the clock back fifty years. The experiment of partition was over, as dead as all the attempts at reconciliation. Not only had the wound re-opened – it was to widen every day in the years ahead.

The Catholics had failed to achieve equality peacefully. Now, in desperation, they were to accept the IRA's attempt to achieve it violently – heralding a programme of shootings, bombings and murder against troops, police and property, often indiscriminate in its killing and maiming of civilians.

It was a pattern of terror accepted by most Catholics, who had so little to lose. In the face of these atrocities the Protestants have only shown such toleration and restraint because they have so *much* to lose.

Internment has been no answer. It alienated the moderates and increased sympathy for the IRA cause.

Direct Rule became a necessity rather than a progressive step to peace. William Whitelaw, appointed Secretary of State for Northern Ireland, was to find that every decision had to be a compromise, too weak in some eyes, too strong in others. He could do no right. It was an unenviable task.

Yet the problem today is the more tragic because it is so understandable, with both sides victims of circumstance like generations of Irishmen before them.

The Protestant feels so British, enjoying all the benefits of British citizenship, that he is willing to fight and die rather than be ruled by a foreign government, an emotion shared by the Catholic, who feels he already *is* being ruled by a foreign government.

And in this terrible stalemate the one true restraining influence is not Westminster, the Police or the Army; it is the very real possibility of civil war which all the time is only hours ahead.

And with every act of violence, moderates are alienated and the polarization to extremism snowballs, while the silent majority gets smaller and smaller every day.

The Calm

The Bogsiders billed it as a peace meeting, held on a football field on 10 August 1969. But the speakers talked of invasion and contingency plans.

Neil Gillespie, a veteran Republican, summed up their feeling as only an Irishman could.

'If we are forced to fight,' he said, 'then let us in God's name fight as peace-loving men.'

In the Protestant Fountains district, the back-to-backs were choked with bunting ready for the Apprentice Boys' Parade the next day. And the man who makes a wet print in a minute was knocking off a foursome. It could have been Battersea or Belle Vue.

12 August 1969

The Parade begins. The Orangemen march erect and solemn. Occasionally there's a brief smile as they spot a friend in the crowd. The beat of the pipe band is lost to the bagpipes that follow behind and they in turn are drowned by the drum band as they take the route that leads them to the edge of the Bogside . . .

At the mouth of William Street, the march is attacked by the Bogsiders.

One man, a catapult, and a marble, said the Scarman Report, may have sparked it all off. Destined for anonymous posterity, he's probably amongst this crowd pushed back down William Street by the RUC, who are abused, stoned and showered with petrol bombs.

It is 3 p.m., 12 August 1969. And it hasn't stopped since.

Against orders from their HQ, the RUC make their first charge into the Bogside, followed by a Protestant crowd.

As they reach the Rossville Flats, they meet a hail of petrol bombs from the roof – it turns them back.

The Protestants turn on the photographers, stoning them against a wall.

I made a run for it, turned into Eden Place and into the first open door. There was an old woman in the hall, in tears. 'When's it all going to end then?,' she kept asking, over and over again.

Weeks later I went back to see her, but couldn't find the street. 'You've got the right place,' a man said, 'but the street's gone; it was burnt down.'

At the junction of Rossville Street and William Street, the Bogsiders erected a solid barricade of flagstones, scaffolding and planks. Then they strung a thin rope across the road in front of it; an Irish mixture of practicality and symbolism.

It became known as Aggro Corner, the centre of the street fighting – no house in the photograph remains standing.

The RUC

◄ *At midnight, 12 August, the RUC got their first CS gas, having relied up to then on stones for defence.*

Within 48 hours they had fired 1,091 cartridges and 161 grenades into the Bogside.

▲

Stalemate on the second morning.

The RUC wear arm protectors, gas-masks, helmets and visors, carry batons and gas guns.

In the background, Rossville Flats are topped by the inevitable frieze of petrol bombers.

▲
One of the 250 RUC injured in the first few days of rioting is helped down Strand Road with a leg injury.

◀ *It wasn't the RUC's stoning or rare petrol-bombing (as here) that shocked; it was their hate that really stunned, matching that of the Catholics.*

The obscenities, the threats, the religious tauntings — and all coming from a peace-keeping force.

To the outsider it seemed so unbelievable.

A constable covers firemen trying to save a blazing house in Rossville Street. Using gas, he keeps the stoning Catholics at a distance.

They light a pile of tyres, but the smoke doesn't carry to the R U C lines as planned. So the Bogsiders advance. It takes a policeman firing continuous gas to drive them back.

The Troops Arrive

On the morning of 14 August 1969 it was obvious to Inspector-General Peacocke of the RUC that the Army must be brought in.

His men, after 48 hours of almost non-stop fighting with the Catholics, were exhausted and outnumbered.

The Bogside was full of rumours of B Specials attacking Catholic homes (rumours stronger, in fact, than the eventual evidence). But the Bogside was boiling for a showdown.

That afternoon Peacocke phoned the Minister of Home Affairs at Stormont and asked for troops. The Cabinet agreed, relaying the request to Downing Street. By 4.30 p.m. Harold Wilson had agreed, and half an hour later the First Battalion the Prince of Wales's Own, on stand-by just outside the City,

drove into Waterloo Place, setting up the barricades.

Their commander, Major David Hanson, tells reporters, 'Provided one is pleasant and polite, one can achieve an awful lot in this world'.

The British Army and Westminster were now totally involved. The Whitehall spokesmen who said they would be back in barracks by the weekend little realized that it would take Westminster years to extricate themselves and their Army from the mess.

It happens so quickly . . .
  This quartet outside a bar haven't even noticed them
march past with barricades.

The arrival of the troops confounds the Catholic crowd. They turn to their stewards. Do they cheer them or stone them? No one knows, but they all seem apprehensive of the rifles.

The stewards are nonplussed. Fearing a confrontation, they form a line and slowly push the crowd back.

A Bogsider watches from the safety of a wall. Another, showing less prudence, climbs a No Waiting sign and holds up his hands at the troops.

I don't know if it was derisive or welcoming. I don't think he knew either.

Weeks before the Parade we had been hearing about the Ulster Special Constabulary, the B Specials, the 'Bully Boys'.

'They'll sort that fucking lot out down there,' they said. 'They won't be shouting so fucking much after a night with the Specials in amongst 'em.'

Their eventual arrival, on 14 August, was an anticlimax. Marching into Waterloo Place in baggy uniforms they hardly appeared the feared force we were promised.

Some carried batons, some were without. They smiled at friends in the crowd, fumbling with handkerchiefs round their faces against the gas. And at the back they struggled to pick up the step.

The B Specials

If the use of the Protestant RUC in the sectarian
fighting was an unfortunate necessity, the mobiliza-
tion of the B Specials for the August riots of 1969
was madness.

While the Catholics had lost any trust in the
RUC, who had already revealed Protestant sym-
pathies during rioting, there was none to lose in the
B Specials – they had been hated for years.

Joining the B Specials was simple – if you were
Protestant. Recruiting was open to any Protestant of
age, without a criminal record. They were immediately issued with a high-collared ex-army uniforms,
dyed black and often ill-fitting; a rifle (sometimes
automatic) which they were allowed to take home
with them, and a nominal salary (about £15 a year
for constables).

They were trained in drill, but were given only

48 hours of weapon training in the first year, and
none at all for riot control.

When, on 13 July 1969, it was decided they should
be mobilized, Stormont insisted they should be
armed with batons only. But it was found there
weren't enough to go round.

Here, then, on the streets of Derry, was a Protestant militia, untrained for the riot control they had
been mobilized for, and tense with fear of a Catholic
uprising.

It was unworkable, unthinkable.

After a few hours' patrolling, wisely confined to
Protestant areas, they were withdrawn, soon to be
disbanded and replaced by a citizen's militia controlled from Westminster, the Ulster Defence
Regiment.

The B Specials had gone. Like so many aspects of
Ulster, it was hard to believe that they had survived
so long.

The B Specials' arrival brings curious looks from the British troops as they march into Strand Road with rifles and sten guns, despite the Scarman Report's assertion that they carried no weapons.

The August Riots, 1969

Two doors from her home, a house blazes.

Forced back by the Catholic rioters, firemen can only watch it burn down.

Advised to leave, she grabs what she can and stuffs it into every drawer, piling it up on the pavement.

Then she carries it away, as the RUC shield her from the stones.

Within weeks, her home had gone as well.

▲ *A rioter soaks the RUC with a fire hose from the Rossville Flats. It isn't effective, but it makes the police look fools. So a crowd gathers to cheer him on.*

He sits provocatively on a fire extinguisher, watching a house in William Street burn down. ▶
  Behind him, the Catholic crowd keep the firemen at bay.

▲

He was found lying in the rubble after an RUC charge. As they carry him to a Bogside first-aid post, someone pulls off his gas mask and asks him where he's hurt – but he's unconscious.

Dead drunk, he tottered between ▶ *the fighting in Rossville Street, with a Quality Street tin on his head and a beer crate in his hand, for protection.*
He, at least, was happy.

▲
Their cursing and taunting has a purpose.

It draws the RUC to within range of the petrol bombers on the roof of Rossville Flats above them.

And, on the left, one man waits for them to draw level, an iron bar in his hand.

You could date this by their faces. Today, children man the barricades. Today the barriers are less permanent. This one, in 1969, was built to keep the Pigs out of Bogside. ▶

And it did.

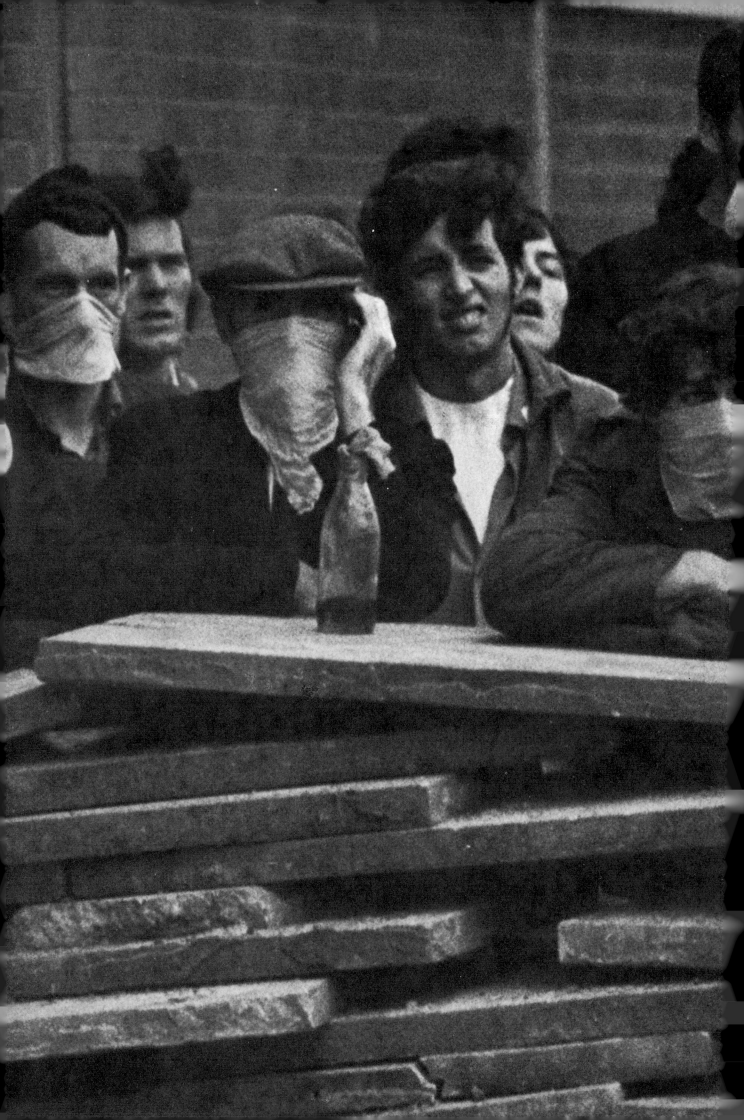

At midnight, they broke down the steel shutters of a bakery in William Street and drove out the loaded lorries, with whooping kids on the running-boards.

The cakes and tarts they couldn't eat they threw at each other in a genuine bun fight. Then a couple of older ones threw petrol bombs through the upper windows until it was just a box of flame. They stood in the middle of the street, chewing and cheering.

The man next to me pointed to the leader. 'You know why he's done that? He went for a job there as a van boy. They asked him which school he went to. He said a Catholic one and they said no vacancies. Can you blame him then? Well, can you?'

The Petrol Bombers

From the shelter of a yard, they lob petrol bombs at the RUC waiting in William Street.

▲
With a cut-away gas-mask and a petrol bomb made from a pop bottle, he waited all afternoon for the police to come within range.

He was about five.

◀
Anticipating the possibility of R U C charges into the Bogside, the Catholics had posted young petrol bombers to the roof of the Rossville Flats.

Girls tore up rags for wicks, the boys filled them and lined them up on the parapet.

And it worked. Every charge was turned back. No one knows how many were thrown down, but that weekend the local dairy lost 43,000 bottles.

Bomber's eye view of the RUC in Rossville Street, standing just out of range . . . a distance learnt from experience.

Amongst the petrol bombers on the Rossville Flats, a boy jerks a stick to his shoulder like a rifle to frighten the RUC below.

Today, it could cost him his life.

The Tricolour and Stars and Stripes fly together from the Rossville Flats.

Ahead of the Catholic crowd, he screamed a short speech of hate at the
RUC before lighting and throwing each bomb.

There was a touch of cinema about it.

The RUC answered half-heartedly with gas and stones, holding their
fire for the next attack by the crowd.

The young bombers soon learnt the danger of long wicks -- they set fire to themselves. It brought rare cheers from the exhausted R U C. ▶

A petrol bomber turns his back on the R U C, weeping with the gas. He carries two spares in the back pocket of his jeans.

Using a low parapet for cover on the roof of Columbcille Court, he scored direct hits on the RUC below.

They tried flushing him out with gas, but the canisters flew over his head.

Finally, they had to rush the flats and occupy the roof. It was the only way to stop him.

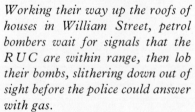

Working their way up the roofs of houses in William Street, petrol bombers wait for signals that the RUC are within range, then lob their bombs, slithering down out of sight before the police could answer with gas.

Direct hits on the RUC's Pigs brought cheers from the Bogsiders, but seemed to cause little injury to the occupants.

Bernadette Devlin

Already she has a following that is more than political.

John Hume, the local M.P., is there, talking sense and leading, but they don't listen and follow in the same way.

She is drab and shapeless, but accepted.

At the height of the fighting, she is close to the front, rallying, cajoling and finally embarrassing the men into action, straining her reedy voice through a faulty microphone.

'For God's sake,' she shouts, 'are you's men at the back just goin' to stand there and leave it to the lads up front? For God's sake, break up the bricks and help them. Or are you's all goin' to just stand there, then?'

It works, but it earns her six months in gaol.

Constituency work.

▲ *All the time, Bernadette Devlin is talking. Encouraging the crowd, arguing with agitators, organising the stewards, then breaking off to hold a press conference.*

Conversation is difficult for Bernadette Devlin and a young petrol bomber. ▶

John Hume

John Hume M.P. is led away from the siege of Rosemount Police Station after being hit by a gas canister: his chief helper shows the presence of mind in the crisis to retain his half of Black Label.

The Catapulter

*He must have been in his fifties, yet he crept into the
backyard with the exaggerated stealth of a scrumping
kid, pulled out a catapult and started firing blindly
over the wall at the RUC behind Bradley's Bar.*

*Few stones reached their target, but it didn't matter.
He was mocking the police.*

The Soldier

'Hey, Tarmmy, you's bastard. Hey, look, here I am you's fucking bastard. Who don't you's fucking well shoot me, you's tartan bastard. You's fucking yeller, that's why, you's yeller bastard. We got one of you's yesterday didn't we, we got one of you's bastards. The fucker was dead before he hit the fucking ground. Did you know that, you's yeller bastard? Hey, Tarmmy, was he a friend of yours, then? Was he a fucking mate, then Tarmmy? Well, you'll have to find another fucking bastard to fuck tonight, then, won't you, you's fucker. Tarmmy, would you like his cap badge, then? Would you Tarmmy, you's bastard? If you fucking want it, come and fucking get it you's tartan bastard. What's up, Tarmmy, you's frightened of using that fucking bastard gun, then? What's up then, you's straight from school, then? We'll teach you's bastards a lesson here, d'ye know that Tarmmy? Hey, Tarmmy, d'you's know what your fucking woman is doing now, do you's Tarmmy? She's being fucked by a big black fucking bastard in your fucking lot. Did you know that, you silly, fucking bastard, eh Tarmmy? Hey, Tarmmy, we's going to get one of you's bastards in the fucking head tonight. D'ye think it's going to be you, you's little bastard? What about that Tarmmy, d'you's want a bullet in your head tonight, eh, Tarmmy? It won't be your fucking mate, will it Tarmmy? We got that fucker yesterday, didn't we Tarmmy?'

For three hours, two soldiers shelter from the stone-throwing crowd at the Little Diamond.

Then one steps out and puts a rubber bullet into them.

Every brick and stone he stands amongst has been aimed at him.

On summer evenings, the sun sinks low and bright through the gaps of William Street houses, burnt down in earlier fighting.

The soldiers dash across these blinding gaps, vulnerable to the stones and nail bombs.

Some wear their cumbersome shin-pads, others settle for copies of the National Geographic rolled down their trousers.

A Pig breaks down; another hooks up, but the towing-line breaks. Suddenly they are encircled by the Bogside crowd. In seconds, they've climbed on top and a man pours paint through an observation slit to blind the driver.

It takes a volley of rubber to break them up; and an officer draws his F N pistol to hold them back.

As soldiers take cover in a row of shops bordering the Bogside in William Street, IRA bombers smuggle 100 lb. of gelignite through the rear of a hardware store.

Suddenly it goes off with a shattering bang without warning. Shoppers run for their lives as the front of the building collapses. Smoke covers everything, and through it comes the strained voice of an officer.

'Sergeant -- What cas.?'

You hear them number off.

'No cas. Sir.'

It seems impossible, for there were a dozen soldiers within ten yards of the bomb, grouped around a Pig.

Then a sniper opens up and the soldiers, shaking off the debris, rush for cover, From inside the Pig, a soldier spots his fire. 'I've got him. The window over that bloody arch.' Their returning fire puffs the mortar around the sniper's position.

As the smoke clears, there's a young man lying on his stomach by the soldiers, with blood from a jaw injury staining his shirt. He pulls himself along with his elbows, still clutching two of the cartridge cases he was collecting when the bomb went off. Ricochets from the sniper spurt the sand around him as he reaches safety.

There is another casualty, a soldier with a head injury. They prop him up and stick a cigarette in his mouth. When the sniper fire stops, they run him to their ambulance and the Bogside crowd jeers.

The Bogsiders edge closer to look at the damage.

'No casualties?,' says one. 'Is that what they say, then? They must be fucking joking. I don't believe those bastards for one bloody minute. There must be three fuckers buried in that lot at least.'

Running for cover, a soldier is felled by a stone from the Little Diamond crowd.

He loses his helmet and riot-shield, but holds his gun tightly.

The crowd cheer, and concentrate their fire on him.

He's told to cover sniper fire from Rossville Street and takes what cover he can behind a bollard in William Street.

There are ten blocks of flats in view, maybe 300 black windows the sniper could be in.

The crowd disperses, but he's still there at dusk. A couple saunter past. The boy bends low and looks along the barrel and asks him what he's shooting. And he hears the girl giggle as they walk away . . .

He watches men drift into Bradley's Bar opposite : he hears them order and he hears them singing and joking.

Then he watches them come out. They swear at him and make jokes about him. They ask him if he's frightened and has he shot any snipers tonight . . .

C S Gas

Dr Ben Corson, one of the co-inventors of C S gas, has called it a service to mankind, a description which hardly tallies with that of the Bogsider, who for three years has been choking, weeping and vomiting with it as it invisibly covers streets, seeping into every room of his home at any time of night or day.

But if you try to imagine the pattern of fighting that would have developed on the streets of Derry since 1969 *without* the use of C S gas, then you are inclined to agree with Dr Corson.

It *has* been a service to the Irish.

Kick and run; kick and run . . . there's always someone ready to boot the gas back at the soldiers before
joining the choking retreat of the crowd.

Some reach the stage where they don't bother to run ▶
from gas any more.
   They crouch, shielding their faces as best they can,
coughing and cursing the soldiers, until it drifts away.

There's a ten-foot wall at the Little Diamond they've got to jump if the gas comes from the wrong direction. The youngest can't make it. They stay on top and just sit out the pain, moaning and choking.

▲ A canister lands in Eglinton Place, aimed at rioters who run safely ahead. Within seconds the street is deserted, but indoors the families are trapped. Sunday lunches break up in panic as the gas fills the little rooms. And behind the doors you can hear the children screaming . . .

◀ The gas-masks are Second World War, few are effective against C S. They probably offer as much protection against recognition as the gas.

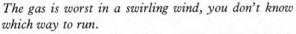

The gas is worst in a swirling wind, you don't know which way to run.

These two have given up the guessing game and sit it out.

Handkerchiefs are little help; CS acts on moisture and you can't wipe your throat dry, or your chest, or your stomach.

To beat the gas, they must run faster than the wind; the more experienced rioters only attack up-wind of the troops.

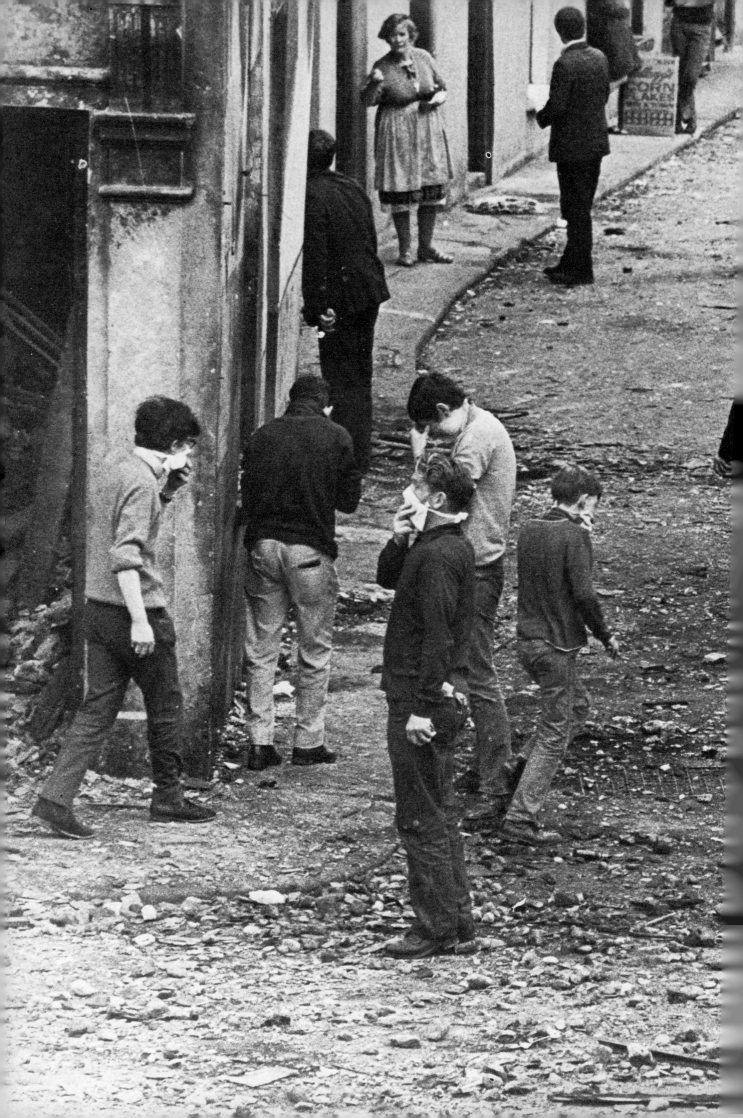

Gas is cruelly indiscriminate.

Within seconds it is invisible and blanketing whole streets, spreading the pain amongst the rioters, shoppers . . . and the lollipop man.

The Gelignite Bomb

A phone call warns the police.

There is a gelignite bomb in the back of a Minivan parked in Shipquay Street. The Army block both ends with land-rovers and a crowd forms behind them, shuffling for a clear view.

They ask about their friends who own the shops around the van, if anyone is working alone and hasn't been warned. The young girls giggle and the mothers jog the babies in their arms. It could be a village turning out to watch the Queen drive by.

Then, in mid-sentence, the enormous explosion, smacking the ear-drums, the image of a fireball, and smoke and debris flying outwards.

The crowd ducks instinctively, then breaks into crouching runs, knocking into each other as they try to shield their heads from the debris — glass, wood and jagged parts of the van. The women are screaming and the children crying.

They straighten up as the debris stops falling, then scatter again, screaming, as a plate-glass window falls out above them.

The soldiers and firemen move in, shouting orders, as the smoke spreads and hangs. Leaves are still falling from the blasted trees.

A curtain drifts down and spikes itself on railings. Within minutes, workmen are clearing the debris and sweeping the streets.

The crowd watches for a while, then breaks up as it's interest dies.

The Hoax Bomb

An anonymous phone call warns the Army of a bomb in the doorway of a bakery.

The calls are regular, maybe once or twice a week. The 'bombs' are usually empty boxes, but it brings the troops into the open to investigate, targets for nail bombs or sniper fire from the Bogside.

But every one must be checked. As the sergeant gingerly pulls the 'bomb' apart, civilians walk past. They know the situation, trust it is a hoax and don't even bother to cross the road.

Within minutes the sergeant calls all clear; a box full of beer cans. The crowd jeers and the stoning begins.

But what of the next 'bomb'? Will that be a hoax? And if it isn't, what of the sergeant, and his mate . . . and the passers-by who pretend it isn't happening?

The Rubber Bullet

For two hours he tries to catch a rubber bullet in the dustbin lid. Finally he does it and even the soldiers cheer. The going rate for them at the time was about £1, mainly to foreign journalists.

9 a.m. in William Street.

The Corporation sweepers are out clearing the barricades, bricks and stones — all the debris of yesterday's fighting.

Only the nails are left, thrown at the soldiers in bombs and embedded in the tarmac by the force of the gelignite.

The stage is ready for today's performance.

He has been ahead of the crowd all afternoon, taunting the soldiers.

The gas doesn't stop him, and as his temper grows so the abuse becomes more vile and personal.

Exasperated, a soldier steps out and fires a rubber bullet into his groin. He collapses and friends drag him out of range.

Forty-eight hours later he was back, and again a rubber bullet drops him. They lead him away, moaning.

Next day he was back, but he doesn't seem worth photographing any more.

The Fighting

His hate, strongest on the day, takes him within a few feet of a Ferret car as it races the gauntlet of William Street.

He screams abuse and hurls rocks at the observation slits. The driver swerves to avoid the dog and you hear him swearing at it from inside. As the Ferret passes, the barrel of the Browning waves menacingly at each knot of young rioters.

They chant,
  'The Daleks are coming,
  The Daleks are coming.'
As Monday afternoons in William Street go, it's fairly quiet.

Maybe it's because they're smaller, maybe the waving Browning barrel incites them, but nothing rouses the crowd so as the Ferrets.

Rioters hold their fire till the very last minute, smashing rocks at the armour as they jump clear; a road accident seems more imminent than any damage from the battle.

Only the dogs enjoy it all.

▲
A hit!

The Little Diamond stoners scream and cheer as a soldier, hit by a stone, is carried away.

It isn't the physical injury that matters – often only superficial – it is the soldier's loss of face that excites them.

◀ *A soldier is attacked at the recreation ground by Creggan Terrace. They snatch his rifle, helmet and riot-shield before he's rescued.*

The rifle isn't seen again, but within minutes the shield and helmet are back on the streets, this time worn by a rioter.

He stands at the front of the crowd in Rossville Street so that the troops can see him. And the crowd cheers and asks the soldiers if they'd like their rifle back.

You know by the cheers a soldier's been hit. He is hurried the length of William Street to a Pig in Waterloo Place. The sight of him silences the shoppers as he passes. It happens nearly every day.

The wire frame has been ripped from a shop front. He holds it up in defiance of the two Pigs, waiting to counter their next run with the boulder in his hand.

It has no effect against the armour-plating, but he will be the last to run.

And that, in his eyes, is enough.

Stoned soldiers can do little to lessen the mood of the rioters. To advance incites, to retreat encourages.

They have to sit it out till the crowd tires, keeping them at bay with gas and rubber. Gradually, the crowd disintegrates, but there is the inevitable boy willing to stay on till darkness, stoning and swearing.

The soldiers don't even waste gas on him. They parry the stones with their shields and just hope he'll go away.

With V-signs and curses, two Catholics try to goad the troops forward into stone-throwing range of the crowd behind them.

The water tank and dustbin lid might stop the rubber bullets, but not the gas; they'll run with the rest when the first canister explodes.

The reaction of a live round.

Even the faces say it wasn't rubber or gas. The unmistakable crack has everyone ducking and running — not to anywhere, just away.

It's incredible how the ear can distinguish and the mind react to the potential danger in a split-second.

There's little consistency in the crowd's reaction to danger.

One day, it will stand it's ground, dodging the rubber and suffering the gas.

Another day, the mere advance of one soldier (in the background, by riot shield) can create such mass panic that they will knock each other over in their haste to retreat.

An onlooker, helping a woman
pinned down by the gas, starts
cursing the soldiers.

They draw batons, hustle him
into the back of a Pig and he's
driven off.

RESIST BRITISH BULLY BOYS!

 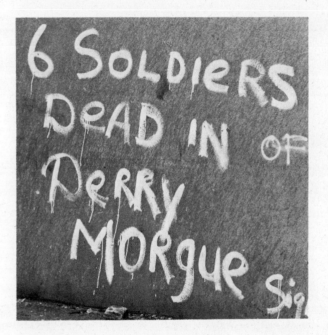

Graffiti

Today the graffiti is everywhere. It is vicious, goading, demanding, philosophical, revolutionary, inciting : it is everything but humorous.

In 1969 I was told of a house with 'Throw Well, Throw Shell' on a wall.

I went to photograph it, but the house was burnt to the ground.

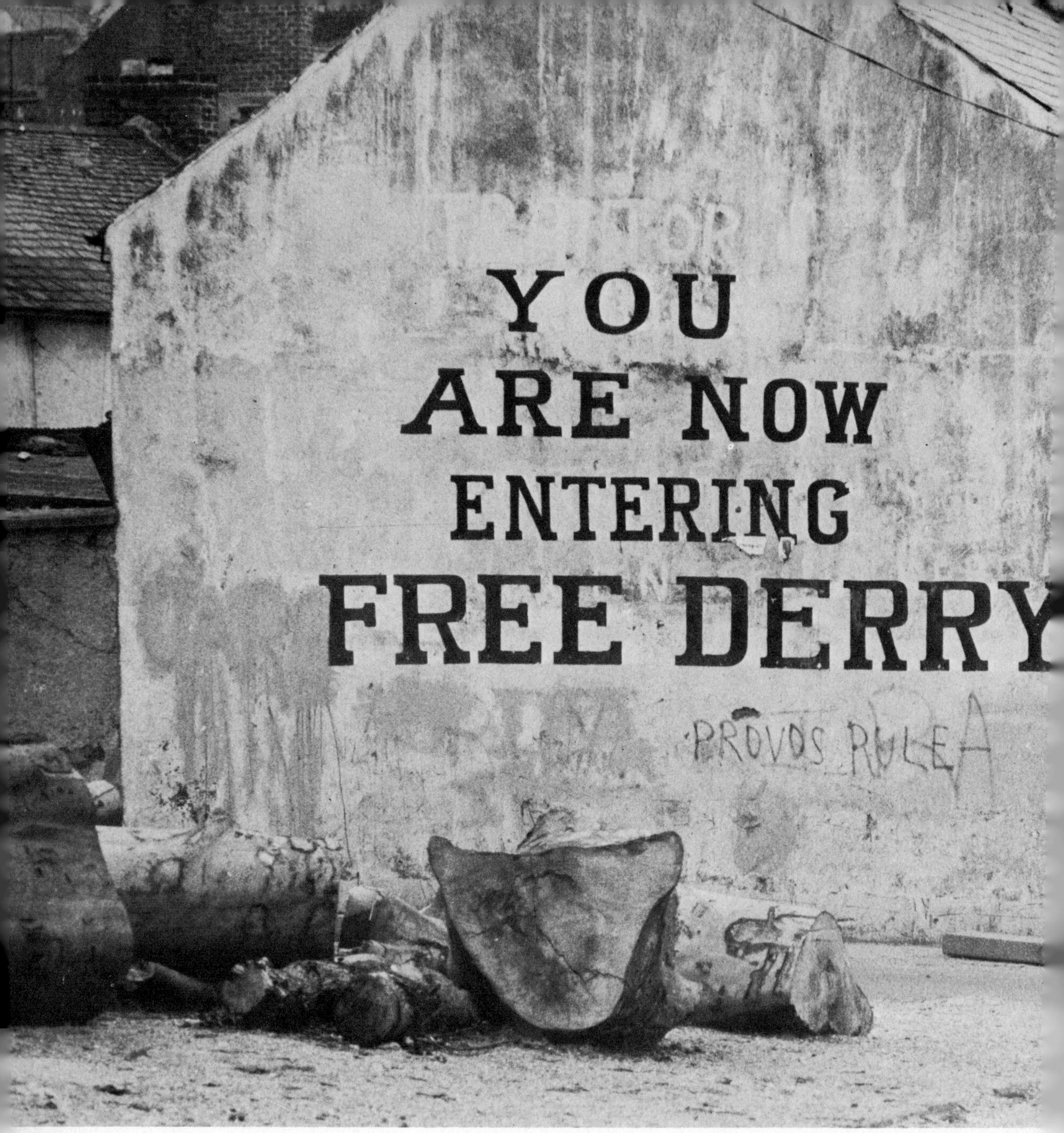

YOU
ARE NOW
ENTERING
FREE DERRY

PROVOS RULE A

Free Derry

Free Derry was born out of a decision of good intent by the RUC in the summer of 1969, that with Catholic feelings running so high against them, they should temporarily suspend their patrolling of the Bogside and Creggan districts.

It was to prove costly, for such short-term solutions in such deep-rooted problems can boomerang, aggravating and increasing the problem in time. And this one did.

Free Derry proved a great physical and political weapon to the IRA, a haven for their terrorists and a bargaining lever against the British government.

It was also a mad anomaly – comic opera if it wasn't in such a tragic setting.

The Catholic inhabitants paid no rates, no fines, no taxes, yet they collected their social security benefits. And the Corporation dustmen still called. On Wednesday nights the bingo bus took the wives to play in a neighbouring hall.

In place of British law, the IRA held their own courts to maintain order. Punishments could be barbaric – tarring and feathering for minor offences; thieves could be shot in the knee, informers in the head. It was a far cry from *Passport to Pimlico*.

Armed members of the IRA cruised the streets in hijacked cars; it was the only indication to the stranger that it wasn't Streatham or Salford.

The British Army's successful invasion of 31 July 1972 ended the three-year existence of Free Derry, this incredible, unique corner of the United Kingdom which was lawless and yet free of bombings and shootings.

It was, as the IRA used to tell you, the safest spot in Ulster.

The Children

Sometimes you watch boys so small that the effort of throwing rocks at the troops lifts them off both feet. They fall pathetically short, closer to them than the soldiers, but it doesn't dim the fury.

'You's bastards,' they shout. 'You's fucking bastards. Why don't you's fucking bastards fuck off then?'

Twenty yards ahead of them are soldiers with loaded rifles. Twenty yards behind a nail-bomber shelters in the crowd. To both sides the boys are an embarrassment, but they stay there.

And you wonder what the hell the parents are doing, what must they be like to let them out, can the desperation be that deep?

If you can understand them, then you can probably understand the rest of the whole bloody mess.

▲

If ever we photographers needed a symbol of the fighting, this was it. Wearing an over-sized gas-mask; a petrol bomb permanently in his hand, so it seemed; and a map of the whole problem on his jacket.

For hours he taunted the police and troops, ignoring the cameras. He was about eight.

God knows what he's advanced to now.

Like a playground activity group, they build a barricade in William Street with the help of a stolen wheelbarrow.

The barricade stops nothing; it doesn't have to. But it brings out the Pigs, sweeping round from the Post Office Depot, a hail of stones clanging off their armour.

Soldiers jump out and, covered by gas and rubber bullets, they roughly clear the barricade with an urgency that comes from the experience of being nail-bombed. Then they are gone, round the corner of Francis Street and out of sight.

Within a minute, as the gas clears, the first boys are back. Within ten minutes, the barricade is rebuilt . . .

And the ritual goes on.

A young rioter, armed with a petrol bomb and a catapult in his back pocket.

The kids soon learn to hold their ▶ *fire until the target comes within range.*

▲
A gelignite bomb has been lobbed into a garage in William Street, used by the soldiers as an observation post.

After the explosion the crowd falls silent, listening for sounds of life. No one knows the injuries, for the injured would be taken out the back.

Suddenly, replacements open up with a volley of rubber into the crowd.

And the boys, passing on their way from school, suddenly find themselves in the firing line.

▲
As they leave their school in Francis Street, a soldier's rifle sticks out from the wall.

This they accept and ignore. Only the gas frightens them.

The Baths Incident

I was covering soldiers being stoned at the baths in William Street. One soldier kept the young crowd at bay by jerking his gun to the firing position as they drew too close.

Then, above the shouting and abuse, a man called into my ear, 'Better move over a bit mate, the lads are going to open up with a Thompson . . . on those bastards down at the baths.'

I didn't look at the speaker, but kept the Nikon trained on the soldiers. The crowd beside me melted and I was on my own.

I moved over a little, still focused on the front soldier, now conscious that I was actually waiting to see if he'd be shot dead. Suddenly, the Thompson opened up, loud enough to be beside me. The soldiers dived for cover.

None were hit, but it did little to ease my conscience. Should I have run across to warn the soldiers? Should I have shouted to them to take cover?

You try to remain impartial, but you cannot avoid involvement.

▲
It's not apathy, nor bravery nor ignorance of the situation.

Yet he walks into the path of sniper fire with more chance of being hit than the soldiers who take cover.

He knows the danger, but it has surrounded him and his home for so long he has come to live with it.

Living with a War

▲
Returning from work, they pass a soldier covering sniper fire from Rossville Street; eyes glued to the ground, they wipe the gas from their faces.
   And the conversation doesn't falter.

A soldier trains his rifle on the Little Diamond crowd. ▶
Amongst them is a nail-bomber.
   But the passerby has seen it all before.
   He ducks under the barrel without taking his hands out of his pockets.
   It could only be Derry.

Misjudging his pace, an old man barely makes the safety of a pub door as soldiers race past, firing gas from the waist to break up a crowd.

They've taken her shopping and helped her over the bigger barricades.

They've warned her that there's more stoning at the Little Diamond.

Ahead, she can see gas filling Creggan Street on her route home and just hopes it will clear by the time she gets there . . .

▲
Between the troops' attacks she comes out of her shop in William Street and sweeps the pavement clear.

It's a losing battle; the street stays carpeted with bricks and stones.

Anywhere else it would look funny. But this is Derry, and it's tragic.

From their school in Francis Street, they have to cross ▶
the fighting in William Street or take a long diversion.
Inevitably, there's gas. One turns back, but the
others brave it, burying their faces in turned-up
collars, moaning and weeping through it all.

Impasse in Francis Street.
The girls wait for the gas to clear and the fighting to stop. They discuss the roundabout route to avoid it, then turn to arguing.
The soldier just watches.

The paper boy spots the soldier
sheltering from sniper fire in church
gates at the Little Diamond.

'D'you want to read about the
shooting, then?' he taunts.

The soldier's answer is muffled
by his mask.

'Shouldn't go up there, love. It's a bit dodgy round the
Diamond.'

She doesn't answer, but stands on the corner of
Rossville Street, listening to the crack of rifles, unable
to make up her mind about a long detour.

It's all such a bloody gamble, anyway.

Collecting children from school, a mother is caught in the cross-fire of stones, rubber and gas at Little Diamond.

She breaks down, shouting for help. The children scream hysterically, trying to hide behind her.

A school patrolman runs across and calls them back. They make a run for it, screaming and moaning with the gas.

She takes them back to the school, and talks them into trying just once more . . .

A line of rioters shelter from rubber bullets behind a TV crew in William Street.

The Press

Perhaps no conflict has ever been photographed and reported with such immediacy and intimacy as that in Northern Ireland.

All factions are conscious of the effect of the press in this struggle where the winning of sympathies, both in Ulster and the rest of the world, is vital.

The covering journalist not only runs the risk of being 'used' in propaganda exercises, but also in creating and prolonging rioting by his very presence.

You can reach a point, in Derry as the crowds drift away from the street fighting, when the remaining rioters are outnumbered by the covering pressmen. It becomes embarrassingly obvious that if we went away, they would too – a feeling justifiably expressed by the stoned soldiers.

Yet it is our job to be present. Ideally we should be as inconspicuous as possible; easier for reporters and still cameramen than the cine and TV crews.

Geographically, Derry is perhaps the easiest area of Northern Ireland to cover, for the arena of violence is so compact, confined virtually to the borders of the Bogside and Creggan.

Until it was bombed in 1972 the City Hotel housed most visiting pressmen, and for three years the scene was very much the same.

They sat around reading newspapers, drinking, waiting for the trouble to start. Parties of tourists used to troop through to the dining room, tripping over the camera equipment on the floor. But that was three years ago, and they don't come any more.

To the outsider, the conversation is cynical; there is an air of detachment. It isn't cynicism, but when you have taken in so much of the fighting, and seen the effects of it all on the people, it creates a numbing depression. What shocked a month ago, no longer jars the mind. It takes more to sicken or stir.

If the detachment is real, then it is necessary – the only workable system. To become deeply involved or partisan is impossible; already some have found the strain of Derry too much, been taken off coverage and returned home. It highlights the plight of the people of Derry who might find the strain too great themselves, but have no other home to go to.

In Derry you hear it said, that the world isn't getting any worse, it's just that news coverage is getting better. It's usually quoted by pressmen. Never the Irish.

Incident at Demesne Gardens

Bligh's Lane Army Post is provocatively sited, dividing the Bogside and Creggan. Almost daily it came under attack from sniper fire and stone-throwing mobs.

Saracens and Pigs come out to break up the crowds with gas and rubber; the pattern was accepted.

But sometimes the ritual was broken . . .

At 9.30 p.m. on 12 August 1971, the patrolling Pigs are stoned as usual.

Then a factory adjoining the Army Post is set on fire. A Saracen swings into Demesne Gardens to break up the jubilant crowd.

It stops at the junction with Creggan Broadway. Troops jump out, firing gas into the crowd which advances on all sides.

But the crowd refuses to break up; an officer orders his men back inside. In their haste, their riot screens jam in the doors. The Catholics see this, and move in.

They break down fencing to use as staves. The abuse turns to war whoops. The troops are trapped outside the Saracen, they draw their batons, their shields crack from the stoning . . . and the screaming becomes animal . . .

The first direct blow stuns a soldier.

His mates try to drag him aboard, but the crowd grabs his legs and wins the tug-of-war.

He's kicked to the ground, pummelled, beaten with the fencing stakes.

Suddenly, there's a single shot — and a scream. Everyone knows it's a live round and they scatter, pushing each other over in the panic.

The dazed soldier runs clear in the confusion, but away from the Saracen.

He realises his mistake and runs back.

They pull him in and it roars away, abandoning helmets and shields. An old man, screaming abuse, gets in the last blow, hurling a plank at the closing doors . . .

At the same moment, a boy staggers towards me, groaning. A girl shouts his name, tries to grab him, but he stumbles past to collapse in a hedge.

He has a bullet in his chest, fired from that one live round. The crowd run to him as they hear her screams, and he's carried into the nearest house.

They move him to another over the back gardens. The crowd re-forms, crowding round the front door, waiting to hear how he is.

A man comes over to me. 'No pictures of his face when he comes out. O.K.?'

They send for their own ambulance.

When he comes out, he's covered with a blanket. He raises his hand in a clenched fist salute. The crowd are silent, but moved.

The ambulance moves off and the crowd drifts apart.

The Cost

The Army say he was armed. His friends say he wasn't.

But he was shot, anyway. And where he fell, in the middle of Lecky Road, they built a little shrine with scaffolding around it and a black flag on top.

On Sunday afternoons, carloads of people would come to look at it.

*Junction of Rossville Street and
William Street, August 1969.*

Junction of Rossville Street and
William Street, May 1972.

'Hey, mister, d'you want to photograph a dead fucker then? We've got a bastard through the head. We shot his fucking head off. Over here.'

The boy was leading me round to Columbcille Court when I saw the soldiers bringing him out on a stretcher. They carried him down an alley and through a burnt-out garage to an army ambulance.

He was dead, covered with a blanket.

The news spread amongst the crowd in Rossville Street.

'What's going on, then?'

'The lads have shot a bastard.'

'Right through the chest.'

'No, it was the head. They shot his fucking head off. That'll teach the fucking bastard.'

A boy held out a cap badge to me. 'D'you want to buy his cap badge, mister?'

'D'you want to photograph his brains, then. All over the fucking pavement then?'

The crowd grew as the news spread. They formed a line parallel with the troops blocking the mouth of Rossville Street.

And the chanting began.

'If you kill a British soldier, clap your hands,
If you kill a British soldier, clap your hands,
If you kill a British soldier, kill a British soldier,
If you kill a British soldier, clap your hands.'

It was the younger ones singing, the older ones craned forward to watch the tension.

'We shot him through the head,
We shot him through the head,
Eee aye addio,
We shot him through the head.'

'Hey, Tarmmy, was he a friend of yours then?' 'Was he then, Tarmmy?'

Bloody Sunday

On Sunday, 30 January 1972, a company of paratroopers, involved in an arrest operation in Rossville Street during a Catholic demonstration, killed thirteen Catholics and wounded another fourteen, in shooting which the investigating Lord Widgery later reported 'bordered on the reckless'.

Thirty-six of the paratroopers ran in front of a low wall at Kell's Walk during the operation, and within the next fifteen minutes shot six Catholics at the rubble barricade that ran across the road at the Rossville Flats.

Where they fell, the Bogsiders erected a wooden cross, held together with rubber binding.

And when you stopped to photograph it, the nearest man would start to tell you the names of those who died, where they fell, and how some were running for safety.

Bloody Sunday, an army exercise that went so terribly wrong, is already part of Irish lore. It will never be forgotten and doubtless never forgiven.

The Solution

1972 was a vintage year for solutions to the Irish problem.

In January Lt.-Col. Colin Mitchell told the *Guardian*'s Terry Coleman that he would send round a list of 100 suspected terrorists. 'And you just start shooting them; by the time you have knocked off ten, take my word for it, the other 90 will be in Killarney. They'll go. They can't stand up to it. So you have solved the problem.' Mad Mitch added a further idea. 'What I'd like to do is to have a machine gun built into every television camera and then say to the IRA, come out and let's talk . . . and then shoot the lot.' After a trial? asked Coleman. 'That would be a complete waste of time,' he replied. 'I can understand, because I've met similar people.'

A month later, the *Daily Telegraph*'s L. Marsland Gander proposed his solution in a *Telegraph* supplement. It was a Great Wall of Ulster, a tall, strong-wire fence as used in 'many safari parks in Britain' to run the full 335 miles frontier between Ulster and the Republic.

In May, General Sir Walter Walker said in a speech, 'I have engaged in campaigns against blacks, yellow and slant-eyes. Why should we have one rule for whites and one for coloured?' 'We have to decide if Northern Ireland is part of Britain or not – and, if so, to act accordingly. We should cut off their petrol, gas, electricity and stop food going in, soften them up and go in; give warning so they can get their women and children clear before we go in – but go in.'

That these ludicrous 'solutions' reach print reflects the fact that no workable ones are being conceived. In the vacuum of sense comes nonsense. Yet, incredibly, these three men speak with military experience. Mad Mitch distinguished himself in Aden's Crater district in 1968, later becoming a war correspondent for Beaverbrook Newspapers and then a member of Parliament. L. Marsland Gander was for five years the *Telegraph*'s War Correspondent, and General Walker is a retired NATO commander in Northern Europe.

Maybe they would all benefit from the experience of Tom Edmondson, a bus driver from Hull. Thames TV, in an experiment for their programme *This Week*, took him and his wife to Belfast for a week, just walking the streets and talking. It was a place he knew of from newspapers and television coverage. But the week completely reversed his earlier opinion 'that the Army should be pulled out and the buggers in Belfast left to get on with it'.

The week had shown him that 'they are just decent, honest people who want to live, and the troops are doing a good job keeping more of them alive than there would be'. He was shocked, though, by the resignation, the casual acceptance of the horrors. 'If the Co-op were blown up in Hull, the *Daily Mail* would be full of it for a year.' Looking at the Ardoyne, with whole streets burnt down, he said, 'People spend bloody months just getting their gardens right, then . . .'

To be there, covering the whole problem, you grow to realise that politically, religiously and economically there is a stalemate. The politicians, threatened with trouble from both sides, are forced into decisions of compromise which inevitably displease, delaying and aggravating the situation. Meanwhile the churches are solidified by the fighting, in itself a tragedy, for the solidification merely strengthens their resolve to defend: it doesn't increase their will to break barriers, to compromise and forgive. The terrible unemployment, the acute poverty and the job discrimination produce an economy which itself helps to widen the gulf between the Catholic and Protestant, and the upper and lower classes. The middle class is disappearing, along with the moderate thinkers. The economic misery must be met, and conquered, with a massive financial injection before you can think of a lasting solution.

In Ulster you see just how thin a veneer of civilization covers the animal in us all, how close the holocaust.

The solution will not be religious, political or economic alone. It must come from within every Catholic or Protestant, a slow burying of the worse traits of human nature.

Northern Ireland needs more Christianity, but not in the name of the churches.

And if time *is* to be the great healer, then it must be measured not in months or years, but in generations.

More about Penguins

Penguinews, which appears every month, contains details of all the new books issued by Penguins as they are published. From time to time it is supplemented by *Penguins in Print*, which is a complete list of all available books published by Penguins. (There are well over three thousand of these.)

A specimen copy of *Penguinews* will be sent to you free on request, and you can become a subscriber for the price of the postage. For a year's issues (including the complete lists) please send 30p if you live in the United Kingdom, or 60p if you live elsewhere. Just write to Dept EP, Penguin Books Ltd, Harmondsworth, Middlesex, enclosing a cheque or postal order, and your name will be added to the mailing list.

Note: *Penguinews* and *Penguins in Print* are not available in the USA or Canada

Agony at Easter

The 1916 Irish Uprising

Thomas M. Coffey

This is an account of the uprising that led eventually to the independence of Ireland. The pitiful band of revolutionaries, scorned by most of their fellow Irishmen, were convinced that through their defeat and deaths they would arouse the Irish people to a victorious fight.

From the first day, when belief in a dream outweighed all military considerations, to the seventh day, when the overwhelmed insurgents were finally defeated, this is the dramatic minute-by-minute story of the uprising in and around the Post Office during the week of siege, vividly reconstructed by Thomas Coffey from personal interviews and painstaking research.

'An extraordinarily readable book and a most moving one' – J. H. Plumb in the *Saturday Review*

'While he sticks to the facts and never allows himself any flights of fancy, his account still reads like a good novel' – Benedict Kiely in the *New York Times*

The Irish

Sean O'Faolain

'A creative history of the growth of a racial mind' – this is Sean O'Faolain's own description of a book in which he has no truck with political events, wars, or rebellions and rejects the popular Irish notion of 'seven hundred years of slavery'.

Many racial, religious, social, and intellectual strands have, over the centuries, been woven into the cloth of Irish genius, and it is Sean O'Faolain's achievement to have disentangled these in a study which first appeared as a Pelican over twenty years ago and has now been largely re-written. The wild, imaginative, disunited Ireland of the Celts, which for years became the fountainhead of Christianity; the intrusion of Danes and Normans, who defied the Irish horror of towns and began to urbanize the island; the years of English ascendency, when new populations and a new language were planted; the upsurge of Irish nationalism and Irish letters after 1800 – all these Sean O'Faolain records, critically and engagingly.

Finally he distinguishes six representative types which have branched from the Tree of Liberty – the new peasantry, the Anglo-Irish, the rebels, the priests, the writers, and the politicians.

Not for sale in the USA

Divided Ulster

Liam de Paor

The violence which erupted in Northern Ireland in 1969 and has been continuing sporadically since then was, in Liam de Paor's opinion, easily predictable from the turbulent history of the region.

The issue of civil rights for the Roman Catholic minority produced widespread sympathy, but this is basically more than just a religious dispute. Almost equally deprived in Ulster are the poor Protestants, yet they oppose the Catholics with as much ferocity as the Paisleyite extremists.

Liam de Paor is the author of several books on Ireland and is a lecturer at University College, Dublin. In this skilful and perceptive analysis he takes us through the long and difficult history of Ireland since the great settlement of the seventeenth century and through the struggle for independence. He shows how the Six Counties came to be treated separately and how the religious divisions of the north have been used as an instrument of policy.

In this Pelican edition Liam de Paor has added an introduction and revised his final chapter to cover the more recent events down to the resignation of Major Chichester-Clark.

'By far the most comprehensive, best written and most rewarding book yet published on the Northern Ireland situation and its full background' – *New Statesman*

'The best short summary of the Ulster problem to appear so far' – *Guardian*

A Penguin Special

Ulster

by the *Sunday Times* Insight Team

This is a revised and extended version of two remarkable articles on Ulster which were published in the *Sunday Times* in November 1971. The report, written by the famous Insight team, was internationally acclaimed and the entire text was read into the United States Congressional Record as 'an extremely valuable record of the development of the tragedy in Ulster'.

The team spent four months on intensive investigation and interviewed generals, civil servants, IRA leaders and ordinary people. From the first stirring of the Civil Rights protest to the rebirth of the IRA and its bloody aftermath, their story dispassionately follows the sequence of events in Ulster and fearlessly exposes the facts of discrimination against Catholics and the ill-defined motives of the Provisional IRA.

Apart from details of the 'hooding' techniques used in interrogation – and first revealed by Insight – many new facts emerge in this Penguin Special, which contains additional material about the reform programme, the role of Whitehall, the effects of internment and the Compton report. But its main purpose is to analyse how social, military and political pressures have built up the most violent post-war crisis in Britain.